LITTLE QUICK FIX:

RESEARCH ETHICS

#LittleQuickFix

LITTLE QUICK FIX:

RESEARCH ETHICS

Cheryl
N. Poth

Los Angeles | London | New Delhi
Singapore | Washington DC | Melbourne

Los Angeles | London | New Delhi
Singapore | Washington DC | Melbourne

SAGE Publications Ltd
1 Oliver's Yard
55 City Road
London EC1Y 1SP

SAGE Publications Inc.
2455 Teller Road
Thousand Oaks, California 91320

SAGE Publications India Pvt Ltd
B 1/I 1 Mohan Cooperative Industrial Area
Mathura Road
New Delhi 110 044

SAGE Publications Asia-Pacific Pte Ltd
3 Church Street
#10-04 Samsung Hub
Singapore 049483

Editor: Alysha Owen
Assistant editor: Lauren Jacobs
Marketing manager: Ben Sherwood
Cover design: Shaun Mercier
Typeset by: C&M Digitals (P) Ltd, Chennai, India
Printed in the UK

Library of Congress Control Number: 2020941907

British Library Cataloguing in Publication data

A catalogue record for this book is available from
the British Library

ISBN 978-1-5297-4367-8 (pbk)

At SAGE we take sustainability seriously. Most of our products are printed in the UK using responsibly
sourced papers and boards. When we print overseas we ensure sustainable papers are used as measured
by the PREPS grading system. We undertake an annual audit to monitor our sustainability.

Contents

Everything in this book!

Section 1   Attending to ethical issues is critical to research.
Becoming familiar with the roles of research ethics, guiding principles, and ethical reviews is a logical place for you to begin.

Section 2   Assessing and mitigating risks to protect participants, researchers, and society throughout the research project is a must! **Distinguishing the unique ethical issues for your research helps you design and conduct ethical research.**

Section 3   Providing full information about your research to your potential participants is essential for ensuring free and informed consent. You also need to consider participant vulnerability and capacity to provide consent to demonstrate the ethical principle *respect for persons* in your research.

Section 4 Preparing for data collection and ensuring privacy is central to maintaining confidentiality. You need to demonstrate the ethical principle *concern for welfare* of those involved in the research and ensure secure data storage of paper and digital files.

Section 5 Detailing equitable procedures is necessary for researchers to demonstrate the ethical principle *concern for justice.* **It's imperative to describe how you will select and treat participants fairly and avoid bias in your research plans.**

Section 6 When your research is finishing, you should take care in planning and implementing appropriate exit and communication strategies with your participants. You want to focus on **reciprocal and respectful interactions to conclude your research studies ethically.**

Section 7 During your research, you should **prepare for a range of ethical issues to arise unexpectedly.** Being able to respond appropriately requires ongoing thought and judgment specific to each research project.

Section

1

Attending to
ethical issues
is critical to
research

What is meant by research ethics?

A

summary

Apply ethical reasoning to the
planning and implementing decisions
researchers make to assess and
mitigate risks to protect participants,
researchers, and society.

Research ethics requires planning

Research ethics requires careful planning before conducting research, ethical actions during research, and appropriate responses to emerging issues. You may be thinking, 'If I plan to do ethical research then it will happen right?' The answer is not straightforward because each research study is unique.

A well-articulated research plan that meets the standards for ethical research is a necessary step before beginning. Yet anticipating all the ethical issues that might arise unexpectedly during the study is unlikely so you must be prepared to respond appropriately throughout the research.

Research involves a plan, action, and response cycle to ethical issues. You need to constantly be assessing and mitigating risks to protect participants, researchers, and society by attending to ethical issues as they arise. And the standards for ethical research? We have guiding principles for researchers to follow and ethical reviews of research plans that can support these efforts.

WHY DO WE NEED RESEARCH ETHICS?

Ethical research is essential because it protects participants, researchers, and society.

Understanding how researchers assess vulnerability and risks is important to balance the kinds of benefits that can come from research.

WHO ARE VULNERABLE PERSONS IN RESEARCH?

Protecting the vulnerable is key to research ethics. It can be difficult to define who is vulnerable in research. **There are many ways persons involved in research can be vulnerable:**

Populations and individuals are seen as vulnerable through clinical assessments or common sense; for example, those that have experienced trauma, those with addictions, disabilities or illnesses, and refugees, are all vulnerable in one way or another.

Vulnerability may be based on age, mental, developmental and intellectual disabilities, institutionalization, language barriers, socioeconomic deprivation, or other factors.

If someone is vulnerable then special protections may be necessary – for example, it is often the case that parental permission is required for participants under the age of 16 but there may be cases where the justification can be made for this to be waived.

WHAT DOES BALANCING RESEARCH RISKS AND BENEFITS INVOLVE?

Benefits usually refer to desirable outcomes for participants, communities and society. Risk, on the other hand, refers to the probability that possible harm may occur. Balancing research risks and benefits involves ethical reasoning and risk management where often there is no clear answer. This balance of risk and benefit requires ongoing thought and judgment specific to each research project.

WHAT PRINCIPLES GUIDE ETHICAL RESEARCH?

The standards for ethical research are guided by three principles. The wording of these principles may appear a little different where you live but their meaning remains the same. It is important that the ethical research principles guide your research planning and implementation.

1 The first ethical principle, **respect for persons**, has to do with the treatment of persons and their data involved in the research process. Key ethical issues involve ensuring free and informed consent without interference or coercions – see Section 3, page 39.

2 The second ethical principle, **concern for welfare**, is about the protection of participants by minimizing harm and maximizing benefits of the research. Key ethical issues involve protecting privacy and confidentiality of those involved in the research – see Section 4, page 61.

3 The third ethical principle, **concern for justice**, refers to the need to treat people fairly and equitably and concerns all who participate in the research. Key ethical issues involve reducing sources of bias in researchers, participants, and designs – see Section 5, page 77.

WHO IS RESPONSIBLE FOR THE CONDUCT OF ETHICAL RESEARCH?

The researcher is primarily responsible and needs to seek guidance when needed. One way we do that is to require researchers to complete a review of their research by an ethical review board.

Ethical reviews of research can occur in several ways:

If you are a **student** your supervisor would likely read your research plan and provide feedback about ethical issues in need of attention.

If you are undertaking **research as part of an institution** such as a research centre or university then you likely need to submit your research plan for approval by an institutional review board – also called an IRB.

If your **research takes place within a community or organization** you might also need to submit your research plan for approval by a community or organizational-based review board such as a school organization or indigenous community.

CAUTIONS!

Plan
to mitigate
ethical issues

Action
to implement
ethical practices

Respond
to arising
ethical issues

Be aware and plan accordingly as ethical reviews can take time to complete and some have strict guidelines and submission deadlines for research approvals.

Consider that ethical issues can arise at any time. **Research ethics involves a plan, action, and response cycle** to realize the standards of ethical research.

1 Can you explain why the **treatment of persons and their data** involved in the research process is an ethical responsibility?

2 Can you justify why researchers must **minimize harm and maximize benefits** in their research?

3 Can you defend the need to **treat people fairly and equitably** as research participants?

4 Can you describe the **role of research ethics reviews?**

5 Can you assess potential **participant vulnerability?**

If you can answer 'yes' to each of these, then you are ready to apply your understandings of research ethics to a study!

Section

Distinguishing the unique ethical issues for your research helps you design and conduct ethical research.

How do I identify critical ethical issues for my research?

A

Outline the why, who, where, how and
what of your research to begin identifying
critical ethical issues in relation to the
guiding ethical principles.

Distinguishing the unique
ethical issues for your
research helps you design and
conduct ethical research.

How do I identify critical ethical issues for my research?

A

10 SEC summary

Outline the why, who, where, how and
what of your research to begin identifying
critical ethical issues in relation to the
guiding ethical principles.

Planning is essential

A well-considered, well-articulated list of ethical issues and plans to mitigate will guide you in the conduct of ethical research. It will help you to identify ethical issues to anticipate and point you to issues that might arise. While it is impossible to anticipate and plan for all scenarios where ethical issues will arise, if you do not know what issues to monitor then you will not be able to respond.

Research can differ in many ways and present unique ethical issues. To help identify critical ethical issues in your research, we describe some of the most common ethical issues that arise from research under the following conditions. These are:

1   Problems that require data to be collected directly from participants and thus require considerations of privacy and confidentiality.

2   Research considered worthy of pursuit where the potential benefits outweigh the risks and thus is committed to equitable and fair treatment of people, communities, and data.

3   Research participants who are legally competent and thus have enough decision-making capacity to consent to research.

DISTINGUISHING UNIQUE ETHICAL ISSUES FOR YOUR RESEARCH

Without clear articulation of our research details and the possible ethical issues we must attend to, it is impossible to plan for them. A well-articulated list of ethical issues relevant to your study provides both you and your readers with information related to the three ethical research principles:

Respect for persons – see Section 3, page 39

- How will you ensure free and informed participation in your research?
- How will you avoid interference or coercions?

Concern for welfare – see Section 4, page 61

- How will you minimize harm and maximize the benefits of your research?
- How will you protect the privacy and confidentiality of those involved in the research?

Concern for justice – see Section 5, page 77.

- How will you treat people fairly and equitably in your research?
- How will you select participants, collect data, and report findings and avoid bias?

RESEARCH PLANS GUIDE ETHICAL RESEARCH

The first step in assessing and mitigating risks to protect participants, researchers, and society is to fully describe our research plans. The questions on the following page can guide your planning and identifying ethical issues in your research.

Answers to these questions are necessary to identify critical ethical issues in need of your attention and are relevant to the three principles of ethical research. It also helps to assure others of your ability to conduct ethical research.

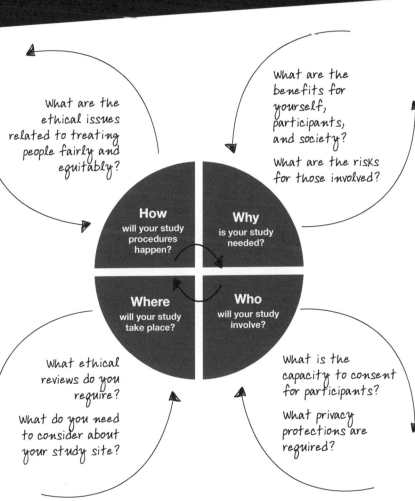

What are the ethical issues related to treating people fairly and equitably?

What are the benefits for yourself, participants, and society?

What are the risks for those involved?

How will your study procedures happen?

Why is your study needed?

Where will your study take place?

Who will your study involve?

What ethical reviews do you require?

What do you need to consider about your study site?

What is the capacity to consent for participants?

What privacy protections are required?

Here are some questions to
guide your research planning:

Why is your study needed?

....

....

Who will your study involve?

....

....

Where will your study take place?

....

....

How will your study procedures happen?

....

....

Now use the following questions to guide identifying
your critical ethics issues in your research:

**What benefits do you anticipate from your research; for yourself,
your research participants, and society?**

....

....

What risks do you anticipate for those involved in your research?

☐ Mental health such as stress and embarrassment
☐ Physical health such as medical burdens
☐ Social wellbeing such as risks to employment

What vulnerability of persons do you anticipate for those involved in your research?

☐ Population characteristics such as language barriers, common experiences, socioeconomic deprivation
☐ Individual qualities such as age, disability, legal competency

How will you protect the privacy of your research participants?

☐ Methods of data collection
☐ Data management and storage

What ethical reviews approvals do you need?

☐ Institutional
☐ Community or organizational

What procedures will ensure the equitable and fair treatment of people in your research?

☐ Participant recruitment and sampling
☐ Data collection and reporting

In the next sections, we will revisit your answers here and create a plan for addressing your critical ethics issues in your research.

CHECKPOINT

Get it?

Q: Why is it necessary
to describe a detailed
research plan?

Got it!

A: To identify critical ethical issues and guide the conduct of ethical research.

I CAN DISTINGUISH THE UNIQUE ETHICAL ISSUES FOR MY RESEARCH AND BEGIN TO MAKE PLANS TO MITIGATE THEM!

. . . .

Section

Providing full information about your research to your potential participants is essential for ensuring free and informed consent.

How do I obtain free and informed consent from research participants?

Fully explain the study, inform
participants of their rights, answer
your participants' questions, and take
care to document consent.

Free and informed consent involves a process that begins before participants are recruited and continues until the end of the study.

Free and informed consent requires careful planning of research procedures, keeping in mind your participants and their capacity for decision-making and providing free and informed consent. By providing their informed consent, participants affirm that they understand the purpose of the research and what their participation in the research involves, and that their decision to participate is made voluntarily and free from coercion.

PARTICIPANT RIGHTS

Potential participants in your research need to know their rights to:

- *Voluntary participation:* Participants are under no obligation to participate or answer questions that they do not want to answer.

- *Withdraw without penalty:* Participants can withdraw at any time and need to know how to do this.

- *Access findings:* If participants will have access to the findings, they need instructions for how to do this.

- *Clarify their understandings:* If participants have further questions, they need to know who to contact for more information.

WHEN AND HOW RESEARCHERS ENSURE FREE AND INFORMED CONSENT?

Researchers can ask themselves the following questions:

Before conducting the research

Does my assessment of the research benefits outweigh the potential risks for participants?

Do my research plans minimize risks and maximize benefits for participants?

Does my assessment of the vulnerability raise concerns about the capacity of my participants to consent?

Do my research plans put in place adequate special protections for vulnerable participants?

Have I prepared documentation and received the necessary ethical review approvals?

Beginning to conduct the research

Am I recruiting participants and explain the study purpose and procedures in ways that are accessible, truthful, and appropriate?

Am I informing participants of their rights related to withdrawing from the study, expectations for privacy, and access to study findings and benefits?

Am I providing opportunities for participants to ask questions and clarify their understandings of the research and their participation?

Am I seeking and document voluntary and informed consent in ways that are appropriate for the research and participants?

During the conduct of the research

Am I monitoring that participants continue to understand the study purpose and procedures and reaffirm their consent to participate and have their data included in the research?

Am I following through on my promises of compensation and/or reimbursement of costs?

Am I collecting and store data in ways that adequately protect participant privacy?

Am I reporting study findings in ways that maintains participant confidentiality?

Have I provided participant access to findings as I have promised?

What does free consent involve?

Participants must voluntarily agree to participate in the research. **A key component of ensuring free consent is informing participants of their rights to ensure their autonomy –** *their right to consent or not.* Even when participants agree to participate, they can withdraw their consent at any time. It is important that participants know how to do this.

Some common research practices include that as part of the recruitment process, researchers explain their rights to participants verbally as well as in writing in a letter of information that is distributed to participants. It is also important to provide opportunities for participants to ask questions.

What does informed consent involve?

Participants must be fully informed of the procedures involved in the research. **A key component of ensuring informed consent is making sure *participants understand what is being expected of them.***

Some common research practices involve, as part of the recruitment process, researchers explain: the purpose of the research, potential benefits and risks, the procedures involved in the research, and how the data will be used and stored. Researchers may do this verbally as well as in writing in a letter of information that is distributed to participants. It is also important to provide opportunities for participants to ask questions.

What does documentation of free and informed consent involve?

There is no hard-and-fast rule about how to document consent. Considerations around how the data is collected and who the data is being collected from come into play. You will need to use common sense, yet it is important to seek and confirm free and informed consent before beginning the research. Knowledge of different ways consent can be documented can help. Here are some common approaches:

- **By signing their name in writing:** When it makes sense you may have the person provide consent in writing by signing (or typing) their name to a consent form.

- **By stating their name verbally:** If the research involves participants for whom writing is a challenge or who are not culturally accustomed to signing their names then you may ask them to verbally communicate a statement that is then audio or video recorded.

- **With an overt action:** If the data is being collected anonymously or the research involves participants for whom verbal and written communication is a challenge then you may ask them to complete an overt action that is recorded appropriately as implied consent.

- **A waiver:** If the research has no other record of participants' identities and where the main risk for potential harm would be their identity then you may document informed consent by having second eye witness.

- **With special protections:** If the research involves participants who are considered vulnerable then a designate may provide consent verbally or in writing on their behalf.

ESSENTIAL COMPONENTS OF A LETTER OF INFORMATION

Study introduction and details

✓ Study title

✓ Name of investigator and contact information

✓ Invitation to participate, purpose of research, and anticipated benefits

Participation details

✓ What data will be collected and methods used

✓ Where and when data collection will take place

✓ How long data collection will take

Data use and risks

✓ How the data will be used

✓ Who will have access to the research data

✓ Possible risks and protections in place

Confidentiality measures and data storage

✓ What identifying information will be collected and why

✓ Where and how data will be securely stored

✓ What form will data be stored and for how long

Research incentives

☐ What opportunities are available to participants and assurance that if a participant withdraws from the study, they should still recieve the compensation or reimbursement of costs incurred

Participant rights details

☐ Voluntary participation
☐ Right to withdraw
☐ Access to findings (if applicable)
☐ Clarify understandings

Completion of ethical reviews

☐ State if any ethical review processes have been completed and contact details for this review

Final instructions to participate

☐ How to access survey or who to contact to participate
☐ How to provide consent documentation
☐ Inform participants to keep letter of information as a record

Write into the spaces below to create your letter of information. In some places there are clues to guide you.

....

(Provide study title)

....

(Name of investigator and contact information)

You are invited to participate in a study about

....

(Describe the study topic)

because you ....

(Specify the criteria for inclusion)

From this research we wish to learn

....

(Describe the study purpose and benefits)

The study will involve

....

(Describe the data methods – survey, interviews, focus group)

The study will take place..

on..

(Describe the study location – e.g. online, on campus, at an office, and provide approximate dates)

And should take appropriately...

(Describe the study duration – minutes, hours, months)

The results of this research will be used to

....

(Describe use of data – for publications, conferences, public talks)

and will be accessible to...

(Describe who will have access – research team members, investigator)

We anticipate the risks of participation to be low however should you experience,

....

please...

(Describe possible risks and what to do if risks occur – list of resources or contacts)

We will take all measures to ensure the confidentiality of your responses by

....

(Describe data storage – where, how, what form, and for how long)

For your participation, you will receive ....

(Describe any research incentives – compensation and/or reimbursement of costs)

Your participation in this research is strictly voluntary: You may withdraw from the project, without penalty, by

....

(Detail how and contact details)

If you should have any questions or concerns at any time about the project you are urged to contact

....

(Describe who to contact for questions and provide details)

The plan for this study has been reviewed by

. . . .

(Describe any ethical reviews completed)

If you wish to participate in this study please

. . . .

(Describe how to access or who to contact – click here, name and contact details)

If you wish to receive a summary of the study findings, please

. . . .

(Describe how to access or who to contact or what contact information to provide)

Practical tips for letters of information and consent forms

- Do not overstate benefits

- Use simple, jargon-free language

- State participant expectations clearly

- Be specific about research incentives

- Explain how consent is documented

For each of the following four scenarios, answer the questions in the flow chart to help you decide the most appropriate way to document consent.

Scenario 1. Research that involves interviews with participants who are engaged in illegal behaviors

Scenario 2. Research that involves conducting a focus group with parents of young children with autism

Scenario 3. Research that involves an online questionnaire collecting data anonymously

Scenario 4. Research that involves a population of women who are not culturally accustomed to signing their names

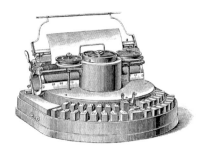

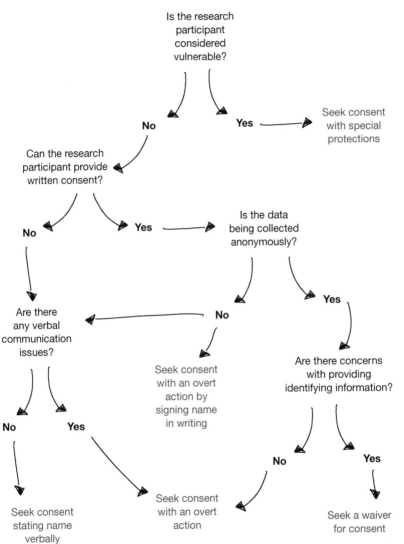

Is the research participant considered vulnerable?

No

Yes ⟶ Seek consent with special protections

Can the research participant provide written consent?

No

Yes ⟶ Is the data being collected anonymously?

No

Yes

Are there any verbal communication issues?

Seek consent with an overt action by signing name in writing

Are there concerns with providing identifying information?

No

Yes

No

Yes

Seek consent stating name verbally

Seek consent with an overt action

Seek a waiver for consent

ANSWERS

CHECKPOINT

1   Seek a waiver for consent. Because the greatest risk for harm is documenting
    their identity, then research is conducted without collecting any identifying
    information including consent documentation.

2   By signing their name in writing. Because the risk is low, then written
    documentation of consent is preferable.

3   With an overt action. Because the data is collected anonymously, consent can
    be implied by the participant consenting to complete the survey.

4   By stating their name verbally. Because the population is not accustomed to
    signing their names, a verbal statement is most appropriate.

Preparing for data collection and ensuring privacy is central to maintaining confidentiality.

1 Section

How do I protect privacy and confidentiality as a researcher?

summary

Assess privacy risks, manage
data with great care, and collect
only what you need.

What are the risks involved with the information you seek?

First, figure out what information you want to collect and the risks involved for participants. Researchers must always consider the potential for a broad range of physical, mental, emotional, social and economic harms from the type of information you seek and the sensitivity of topics you study.

Then work out the necessary procedures for protecting participant privacy and confidentiality while doing and reporting your research. Managing identifying information carefully and collecting only what you need are key to demonstrating the ethical principle *concern for welfare* of those involved in the research. It will be easiest if you can collect your data anonymously – that is without collecting identifying information.

DISTINGUISHING PRIVACY AND CONFIDENTIALITY

Privacy

↳ refers to protecting individuals involved in research

Confidentiality

↳ refers to protecting information or data shared with researchers

HOW CAN RESEARCHERS PROTECT PARTICIPANTS' PRIVACY?

Assessing risks and careful preparation for data collection and use is essential to protecting the privacy of individuals involved in the research. The following can provide some guidance:

Assess, communicate, and take all reasonable measures to maximize potential benefits.

- Do not overstate benefits in the letter of information.

Collect only the information you need.

- Limit the number of sensitive questions you ask.

Plan data collection location carefully.

- Avoid noisy public locations but ensure safety and a private conversation.

Explain how the data will be used.

- Be upfront about where and how the research will be shared.

Become familiar with local privacy laws.

- Report a breach to the appropriate authorities if it happens.

HOW CAN RESEARCHERS MAINTAIN DATA CONFIDENTIALITY?

Assessing risks and attentive data management is central to maintaining confidentiality of the research data. Data management requires close attention to recording, storing, analyzing, interpreting, sharing, and publishing data practices and policies. The following can provide some guidance:

Assess, communicate, and take all reasonable actions to mitigate foreseeable risks to confidentiality.

- Clearly state what data will be collected and detail storage procedures in the letter of information.

Collect only the identifying information you need.

- Avoid collecting personal information if possible.

Plan data management and storage of paper and digital files carefully.

- Remove personal identifiers from the data as soon as possible and secure master list.

Present data in reports in ways that prevents individual participants from being identified.

- Pay attention to the contextual details when publishing.

TO COLLECT ANONYMOUS DATA OR NOT?

It can be difficult to collect truly anonymous data because by definition **data is anonymous *only* when there are no links to any participant identifiers**. In other words, the identity of the participant cannot be known through the data they provide.

Anonymous data is *only possible* when the following conditions are met:

- Participants' identifiers are not needed to answer research questions.

- Researchers do not interact with participants in person or record images or voices.

- Research design does not require data to be linked across multiple participant data sources or interactions.

PRACTICAL TIPS FOR PROTECTING PRIVACY AND CONFIDENTIALITY

- Be specific about privacy and confidentiality limitations.

- Use simple, jargon-free language.

- Collect data anonymously when possible.

- Provide training for researchers who are data collecting and have data access.

- Limit the number of people who have data access.

- Attend to local and federal regulations around data storage.

CHECKPOINT

DO YOU HAVE ADEQUATE PRIVACY AND CONFIDENTIALITY PROTECTIONS IN PLACE?

Ask yourself the following questions.

Does your **research collect information that could be considered sensitive or private?** That is, does your research pose risks to participants that is greater than what they would experience in everyday life?

If yes –

What protections do you have in place for your participants – what questions do you ask and how confident are you that other participants will not share information discussed with others? Look back to your risk assessment at the end of Section 2 – have you covered them all as well as any newly identified risks?

If no –

What is your rationale that your research is of low risk to privacy and confidentiality? If you discover that people are not willing to provide the information you had planned, you may need to rethink your research question and data procedures.

2 Does your **research collect identifying information** about participants? That is, does your research collect participant names, birthdates, email address, phone numbers or anything else that could potentially identify participants if used in combination?

If yes –

What protections do you have in place for your participants – when do you remove identifying information and how are the master files stored? Look back to your risk assessment at the end of Section 2 – have you covered them all as well as any newly identified risks?

If no –

What is your rationale that your research collects only anonymous data? If you discover that your data is not truly anonymous as you had planned, you may need to rethink your data collection procedures.

3 Does your **research identify potential locations for data collection** consider privacy needs? That is, does your research location limit the possibility that others will see participants taking part in research activities or will hear the information being shared?

If yes -

What protections do you have in place for your participants – where do you propose collecting data? Look back to your risk assessment at the end of Section 2 – have you covered them all as well as any newly identified risks?

If no -

What is your rationale that your research location allows for privacy? If you discover that your location is not as private as you had planned, you may need to rethink your research locations.

4 Does your **research plan specify who will have access to the data and in what form?**

If yes –

What protections do you have in place for your participants – have you removed all identifying information before sharing? Look back to your risk assessment at the end of Section 2 – have you covered them all as well as any newly identified risks?

If no –

What is your rationale for who will have access to what data? If you discover that the risks to sharing data with others is greater than you had planned, you may need to rethink the form of the data you share.

Overall, if you can answer 'yes' to each of these then you have planned a study that attends to the privacy and confidentiality needs of your participants and data.

Section

5

It's imperative to describe how you will select and treat participants fairly and avoid bias in your research plans.

How do I design equitable research procedures?

You should explain how
your procedural decisions
treat those involved in your
research fairly and avoid bias.

Demonstrating the ethical principle *concern for justice* requires thoughtful attention to the fair treatment of those involved in the research.

Designing equitable procedures involves avoiding bias throughout the research. Bias can occur across the research process and researchers must intentionally engage in efforts to enhance equity because bias is impossible to eliminate. There are three main sources of research bias: researchers, participants, and designs. Reflexive practices can help researchers examine their own backgrounds and biases to understand their effect on research decisions. Careful attention to sampling strategies can help the fair selection of research participants. Considering community norms and potential participation barriers can inform more equitable research designs.

Designing equitable procedures is essential for generating ethical and socially relevant research. Your designs should not perpetuate inequalities and biases that may exist in published research. Designs that enhance the equitable treatment of those involved in the research can provide important guidance for other researchers.

WHAT ARE COMMON SOURCES OF RESEARCH BIAS?

Research bias has many sources. To begin to unpack the common sources of bias in your research, ask yourself the following questions and then read the next sections for guidance.

Researcher

To what extent am I aware of the affect of my own assumptions and biases on my research decisions?

Participants

To what extent does my research sample reflect equal opportunities to participate?

Designs

To what extent do my research designs reflect equitable procedures?

WHAT CAN RESEARCHER REFLEXIVITY CONTRIBUTE?

Reflexivity is an active, ongoing process of examining oneself as a researcher and how one's assumptions and preconceptions affect our research decisions. Reflexivity is the process of becoming self-aware of one's potential and real biases. It can help researchers understand how their structural, political, and cultural environments (among others!) affect the research process and outcomes.

Reflexivity can help prepare researchers for many 'ethically important moments' that will arise in the day-to-day life of a researcher. It can also help researchers to engage in equitable and respectful research, which in turn can generate more ethical and socially relevant research approaches and outcomes.

As a starting point, the following can be helpful questions for researchers to consider:

To assess shared personal identities related to this study:	To identify motivations for study involvement:
Which identities do you share (or not share) with your participants?	Why pursue the problem addressed by your study?
How do the common and different identities affect the way in which participants might interact with you as the researcher?	To what extent do personal identities lead you as the researcher to look for specific things?
How might the interactions influence the information participants share?	Could your personal motivations lead you to draw specific conclusions?

WHAT DOES FAIR TREATMENT MEAN?

Fair treatment can involve providing equal access to both the research benefits and potential risks. This can influence how participants are selected and how findings are shared. It can also refer to the need for collecting data in ways that are appropriate for the participants, the researcher, and the study problem pursued. It is important that the data procedures follow the practices related to free and informed consent and protecting the privacy and confidentiality of those involved. It is also essential that the decisions guiding data procedures consider participant characteristics that would hinder and support participation so that all voices can be represented in our societal research.

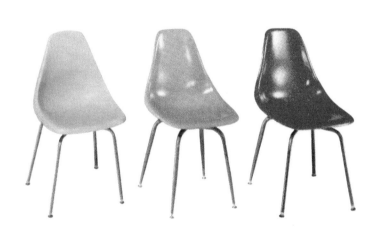

ENHANCING EQUITY IN YOUR RESEARCH DESIGN

Research designs provide many opportunities for enhancing equity in the procedures. To start your thinking, ask yourself the following questions about the different stages of the research process:

Recruiting Plans

Do I recruit participants in ways that are equitable and appropriate?

Do I clearly rationalize who I am involving in the research and any potential participation barriers?

Sampling Participants

Do I clearly define my inclusion and exclusion criteria for participation?

Are the risks and benefits distributed equitable among those involved in the research?

Collecting Data

Do I collect data using methods and protocols that are appropriate for participants and communities?

Do I collect data in ways that minimize disruption and burdens?

Generating Inferences

Do I represent study findings in ways that are accurate and respectful of participants?

Do I gather evidence from participants that my interpretations are accurate?

Accessing Findings

Do I share study findings in ways that are accessible and beneficial to participants?

Do I bear in mind the potential impacts of my study on participants?

PRACTICAL TIPS FOR EQUITABLE RESEARCH DESIGNS

- Unpack any assumptions and address the biases you bring to your research.

- Clearly define your participant inclusion/exclusion criteria.

- Mitigate potential barriers to participation in your research.

- Justify your data procedures keeping in mind participant characteristics that may prevent participation.

- Engage communities as partners in data analysis to avoid misinterpretations.

- Ensure equal participant access to your research benefits.

ENHANCING EQUITY IN YOUR RESEARCH STUDY

DO IT YOURSELF

Write in your answers related to your research study. In some places there are clues and questions to guide your design justifications.

A. My participant recruitment strategy

I will recruit my participants using

....

(A poster/social media/email/personal contacts)

because

....

(Describe why this is appropriate for your research and participants.)

Participants might not be able to participate because

....

(Describe what barriers your research participants might face, e.g. lack of childcare or technology access, transportation costs.)

90

What are three things you can do in your participant recruitment strategy to enhance your demonstration of the ethical principle concern for justice?

1 ....

2 ....

3 ....

B. My participant sampling plans

I will choose my participants based on the following criteria for selection

....

(Specify population or individual characteristics.)

because

....

(Describe why this is important for your research.)

Participants might not choose to participate because

....

(Describe what risks your research participants might face - e.g. time burdens, invasion of privacy, economic, social, mental harms.)

HOW TO ESTABLISH EQUITABLE ETHICAL RESEARCH

What are three things you can do in your participant sampling plans to enhance your demonstration of the ethical principle concern for justice?

1 ....

2 ....

3 ....

C. My data collection procedures

I will collect my data using

....

(Specify data collection methods or protocols.)

because

....

(Describe why this method or protocol is appropriate for your research and participants.)

Participants might not be able to participate because

....

(Describe what burdens your research participants might face – e.g. language, cultural norms, accessibility.)

What are three things you can do in your data collection procedures to enhance your demonstration of the ethical principle concern for justice?

1 ....

2 ....

3 ....

D. My inference generation approach

I will interpret my data using

....

(Specify data analysis methods or protocols.)

because

....

(Describe why this strategy is appropriate for your research and participants.)

Participants might be concerned about

....

(Describe what concerns your research participants might have – e.g. privacy, how the findings are represented and used.)

93

What are three things you can do in your inference generation approach to enhance your demonstration of the ethical principle concern for justice?

1 ....

2 ....

3 ....

E. My findings communication plans

I will share my findings with my participants using

....

(A presentation/email/written report.)

because

....

(Describe why this is appropriate for your research and participants.)

Participants might be interested in the findings because

....

(Describe what contributions your research might make –
e.g. theoretical, practical, methodological.)

What are three things you can do in your communication plans to enhance your demonstration of the ethical principle concern for justice?

1 ....

2 ....

3 ....

I CAN NOW PLAN RESEARCH THAT MEETS THE THREE GUIDING ETHICAL PRINCIPLES: RESPECT FOR PERSONS, CONCERN FOR WELFARE, AND CONCERN FOR JUSTICE!

....

#LittleQuickFix

Section

6

Focus on reciprocal and respectful interactions to conclude your research studies ethically.

How do I conclude research projects ethically?

You should look after yourself and your participants and their interests.

Be reciprocal-minded, respectful, and ethical

There is no hard-and-fast rule about how to conclude a research project ethically. You will need to use common sense and care in planning and implementing appropriate exit and communication strategies for concluding your research. As part of the free and informed consent process you entered an agreement with your participants to respect their rights and boundaries you set with participants and communities.

Conducting yourself ethically as you conclude your research is important to fulfill your mandate to protect participants, yourself, and society. An ethical researcher will treat participants fairly and have participants and their own wellbeing in mind beyond the particular study.

WHAT DOES AN ETHICAL EXIT STRATEGY INVOLVE?

An ethical exit strategy should reflect a thoughtful plan for guiding how you will conclude your research and your interactions with participants. There are many ways you can go about this. This may involve providing access to the research findings and benefits in ways that make sense for your participants.

Remember your participants have agreed to be involved in the research according to the participation expectations stated in the letter of information. In the same way, if you have fulfilled your expectations as a researcher then you should feel free to move onto your next project. If your ethics review approval requires a final report then get it done.

QUESTIONS TO GUIDE AN ETHICAL EXIT STRATEGY

One way to think about an ethical exit strategy is to ask yourself four guiding questions:

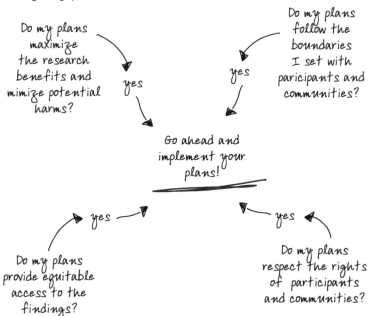

Do my plans maximize the research benefits and mimize potential harms?

yes

Do my plans follow the boundaries I set with paricipants and communities?

yes

Go ahead and implement your plans!

yes

Do my plans provide equitable access to the findings?

yes

Do my plans respect the rights of participants and communities?

HOW CAN RESEARCHERS CONCLUDE STUDIES RESPECTFULLY?

To respect the rights of participants it is necessary that you confirm, at the end of the study, that you have fulfilled the agreements you made at the beginning related to:

✓ Did the participants participate voluntarily in the research?

✓ Did you honour any participant's request to withdraw from the research?

✓ Did you provide participants with access to the study findings and research benefits?

✓ Did you adequately respond to participants' questions throughout the research?

RESPECTING BOUNDARIES SET WITH PARTICIPANTS?

It is **important that you do not burden participants beyond their agreed upon expectations**. In the same way, if you said you would share study findings with participants, then start planning how this will happen – a public presentation? An email with a written summary? If you said you were going to publish, then do all you can to see through this expectation. In all these activities it is important that you continue to protect privacy and confidentiality, present findings honestly and accurately, and give credit to authors as you have agreed to do.

CONTRIBUTING TO SOCIETAL SUPPORT OF RESEARCH

Because researchers have an ethical responsibility for the wellbeing of themselves, their participants, and society, it presents an opportunity for researchers to enhance understanding of the role research contributes to society betterment. This can translate into support for institutions, organizations, and community capacity for research and funding. The impacts are further augmented since reciprocal-minded, respectful and ethical research can encourage involvement as future research participants and use of equitable designs that others can learn from.

PRACTICAL TIPS FOR CONCLUDING RESEARCH ETHICALLY

- Clearly communicate your exit strategy.

- Fulfill agreements you have made.

- Respect boundaries you have set for participants.

- Avoid further burdens to your participation.

- Encourage reciprocal learning from the research.

- Disseminate your research so others can build upon it.

Get it?

Q: If you asked a researcher to explain what ethical research is, what would be a good answer?

Got it!

A: A researcher who pays attention to ethical issues throughout their research and beyond!

Section

7

**Prepare for a range of
ethical issues to arise
unexpectedly.**

What are the practicalities of responding to ethical issues as they arise?

Consider when and what
ethical issues may arise, and
how best to respond.

Anytime, anywhere, in many ways

Ethical issues reside across the research process. Research does not always unfold as planned. It is crucial for researchers to continually attend to ethical issues throughout their research project. Even with careful planning, researchers may encounter new ethical issues after a project is in progress that requires decisions about how to proceed.

WHAT CAN GUIDE RESEARCHERS' APPROACH TO ARISING ETHICAL ISSUES?

All researchers need to be prepared to respond appropriately when issues arise – researchers can be guided by careful planning to pay attention to changes, take actions to identify arising ethical issues, and respond in a way that meets the three guiding ethical principles.

What changes in the research have occurred to the PLAN?

What ethical issues need ACTIONS by the researcher?

What researcher RESPONSE is warranted?

Is it about the treatment of persons and their data?

Is it about the protection of those involved in the research?

Is it about the need to treat people fairly and equitably?

Research contexts are dynamic and subject to changes that are beyond your control. Thinking ahead to the ethical issues raised by procedural changes can help you respond appropriately. **Considering common changes that occur in research can help prepare researchers for many of the arising ethical issues.**

It is hard to predict but examples of issues that can arise and require our attention involve:

Our instruments or protocols creating unintentional participation barriers

✓ For example, our scheduling of focus groups meant participants without childcare access could not attend.

ANTICIPATING ETHICAL ISSUES

A question was inadvertently distressing to participants

✓ For example, a question about childhood triggered a traumatic response.

Our participants experiencing interference in their participation

✓ For example, our participants were subtly coerced by their boss.

Our participant relationships extending beyond the study scope

✓ For example, our participants wanting to remain in contact beyond the study.

For many issues, there is no clear right or wrong answer about how to respond. To help you weigh your options, you may wish to engage in ethical reasoning which you were introduced to in the first section.

What is important is to take the time to carefully consider your options and then discuss the options with someone who is guiding you in your research. This can help you make the best decision possible for your specific circumstance.

RESPONDING TO ETHICAL ISSUES ON-THE-GO?

Sometimes changes you make to a research plan have ripple effects on any approvals from ethical review boards. For example, if you change how you planned to recruit participants – from using a posted sign in a community hall to using an email listserve – then it is important to tell those who are guiding you in your research about these changes. Sometimes you will be required to submit an updated research plan to your supervisor or an amendment for approval to an ethical review board before you begin. Be sure to ask questions and inform yourself.

WHAT *ELSE* MUST RESEARCHERS CONSIDER WHEN RESPONDING TO ARISING ETHICAL ISSUES?

Circle 'yes' or 'no' in response to the following statements.

I have identified some changes to my plan that could occur during my research.   YES / NO

I have worked out what actions would be necessary for me to do.   YES / NO

I have identified the ethical issues that would arise.   YES / NO

I have identified the ethical principles I need to address.   YES / NO

If you can say 'yes' to all four - you have planned your practicalities!

Anticipating ethical issues is key to managing and mitigating them as they arise.

DID YOU KNOW?

**CONGRATULATIONS!
YOU ARE READY TO CONDUCT
ETHICAL RESEARCH.**

**USE THE GUIDANCE IN THIS
BOOK TO PROTECT YOUR
PARTICIPANTS, SOCIETY, AND
YOURSELF.**

#LittleQuickFix

Work through this checklist to help ensure you have mastered all you need to know to conduct ethical research:

☐ Can you explain the roles of research ethics, guiding principles, and ethical reviews? If not, go back to page 9.

☐ Have you identified the unique ethical issues for your research? If not, go back to page 23.

☐ Do your research plans ensure free and informed participant consent? If not, go back to page 39.

☐ Have you made plans to maintain confidentiality in your research? If not, go back to page 61.

HOW TO KNOW
YOU
ARE
DONE

☐ Do your sampling and research procedures demonstrate evidence of equity? If not, go back to page 77.

☐ Have you considered how you will conclude your research study ethically? If not, go back to page 101.

☐ Have you considered the range of ethical issues that may arise unexpectedly during your research? Are you prepared to respond appropriately? If not, go back to page 115.

Glossary

Benefit   A desirable outcome for individuals or society, such as useful information or betterment.

Confidentiality   The obligation to keep some types of information confidential or secret.

Consent form   Documents, in writing, a research participant's informed decision to participate.

Data management   Practices and policies related to recording, storing, auditing, archiving, analyzing, interpreting, sharing, and publishing data.

Ethical reasoning   Making a decision in response to a moral dilemma based on a careful and thorough assessment of the different options in light of the facts, circumstances, and ethical issues.

Ethical review   A process intended to protect research participants by minimizing the harms or risks to which they are exposed during research activities. Often takes place within a community, an organization, or an institution.

Implied consent   Occurs through the actions or conduct of the participant rather than signing their name.

Informed consent   The process of making a free and informed decision such as to participate in research. Individuals who provide informed consent must be legally competent and have enough decision-making capacity to consent to research.

Interference   Use of coercion, threats, or intimidation to make a person comply with a demand, such as to participate in research.

Justice   An ethical principle that obligates one to treat people fairly.

Letter of information   Provides information in writing about the purpose of the research, the research procedures involved in participation, potential risks and benefits of the research, and details about rights of participants and withdraw procedures.

Reflexivity   An active, ongoing process of engaging in critical reflection of how the researcher constructs knowledge from and during the research process.

Research ethics   The application of fundamental ethical principles to the planning and implementation of research. Researchers are often guided by three principles for conduct of ethical research: respect for persons, concern for welfare, and concern for justice, which require ongoing thought and judgment specific to each research project.

Respect for persons   A moral principle that researchers should respect the choices of autonomous decision-makers and that researchers should protect the interests of those who may be vulnerable.

Risk management   The process of identifying, assessing, and deciding how best to deal with the risks of a research activity.

Vulnerable research participants   Participants who have an increased susceptibility to harm or exploitation due to their compromised ability to make decisions or advocate for their interests or dependency. Vulnerability may be based on age, mental disability, institutionalization, language barriers, socioeconomic deprivation, or other factors.

Withdrawal   From research refers to the rights of participants to voluntarily remove their data from a study or be withdrawn by the researcher to protect them from harm or ensure the integrity of the study and request data be removed.